PICTURE THE WORLD
FARM MACHINES

AWARD PUBLICATIONS LIMITED

The bulldozer

A bulldozer is a tractor specially designed for clearing and levelling land before crops are planted. It has a very powerful engine, caterpillar tracks rather than wheels, and a curved shovel blade at the front which can be lifted and forced down by its strong mechanism. The shovel is used for moving earth, large rocks and tree-stumps and then levelling the land.

The tractor

Tractors can be found on farms of every size all over the world. Whether it is a dairy-farm, or a sheep-farm, or a farm growing crops of some kind, you are sure to find a tractor working there. Tractors are used for pulling other farm machinery and travelling over rough and muddy ground. In this picture the tractor is being used to take food to sheep in a mountainous area.

Ditch digger

ISBN 0-86163-966-9

Copyright © 1999 Award Publications Limited

First published 1999
Second impression 2002

Published by Award Publications Limited,
27 Longford Street, London NW1 3DZ

Printed in Singapore

The baler

After the crops have been harvested and the grain has been separated from the stalks, a baler is used to gather up the stalks into round or oblong bales which are then banded. These bales of straw are taken to the farm and stored for use as winter bedding for the animals.

Harvesting the crops

At harvest time the farmer gets out his biggest machine, the combine harvester. This slowly rolls across the field, cutting and threshing the wheat as it goes. This separates the grain from the 'ear' at the top of each stalk. The grain pours down a spout into the grain trailer which takes it to the farm for storage. At the same time the stalks are pushed out of the back of the combine harvester to be collected by a baler.

Crop-spraying

Once the crops have grown to a certain height, they are sometimes sprayed with chemicals that will protect them from attack by pests that might cause damage or destroy them. To do this, a tractor pulls along a tank of the pest-killing chemical and sprays it on to the crops. As it is dangerous to inhale chemicals of this sort, the farmer will wear a protective mask when he is doing this work.

Sowing the seed

In the autumn, after ploughing the land, the farmer sows the seeds for the following summer's harvest. The tractor pulls a large container which holds the seeds and an enormous rake which runs through the earth. As the rake moves along the seeds fall into the ground through funnels leading into the rake.

The plough

Until about sixty years ago heavy horses or oxen, led by men, were used to pull the plough across the field turning over only one furrow at a time. Today, ploughing the land is much quicker as a tractor is used to pull the plough, which can turn over six or more furrows at a time. The blades can be turned over at the end of a furrow for ploughing in the opposite direction.